Phonics
Practice Book

Grade 1

Harcourt School Publishers

Visit The Learning Site!
www.harcourtschool.com/storytown

ISBN 10 0-15-358738-5

ISBN 13 978-0-15-358738-2

10 11 12 13 14 15 0982 15 14 13 12 11 10

Contents

Level 1-1

Lesson 6

Level 1-2

Lesson 7

Lesson 8

Lesson 9

Lesson 10

Cut-Out, Fold-Up Books

Name _____

Help the 🐱 get to the ▱. Color the pictures whose names have the short **a** vowel sound.

1

Name _____

c**a**t

Write **a** to complete each picture name that has the short **a** sound. Then trace the whole word.

1	2	3
p a n	h _ t	b _ s

4	5	6
d _ g	h _ m	c _ p

7	8	9
f _ n	s _ x	b _ t

10	11	12
m _ n	m _ p	c _ n

© Harcourt

Short Vowel: / a / *a* • Write Words

Phonics Practice Book

Name _____

cap   ham   map   cat   tap   mat

1.

_____

cap

2.

_____

3.

_____

4.

_____

5.

_____

6.

_____

Name _____

Say the name of each picture. Trace the first letter.
Then use the other letter sounds to complete the word.

1	2	3
s	m	c

4	5	6
m	t	h

7	8	9
p	h	c

Short Vowel: / a / a • Write Words   Phonics Practice Book

cat

cats

If a picture shows more than one, add **s** to its name. Then trace the whole word.

1	2	3
mats	hat	cat

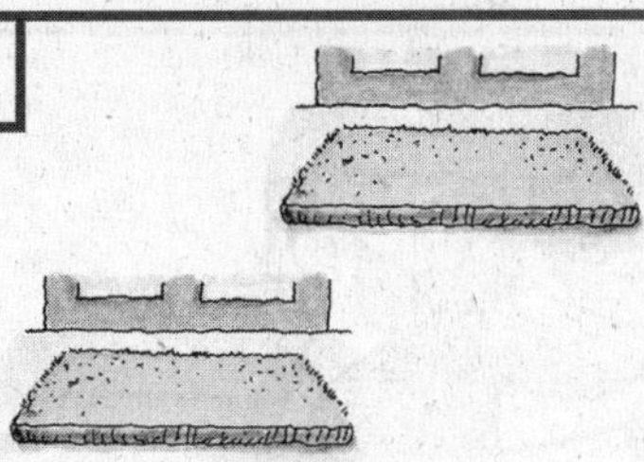

4	5	6
map	cap	hat

7	8	9
ham	cap	map

Inflection: -s • Write Words

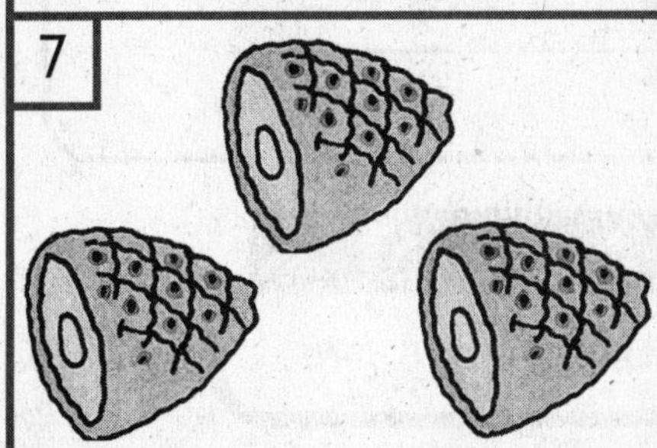

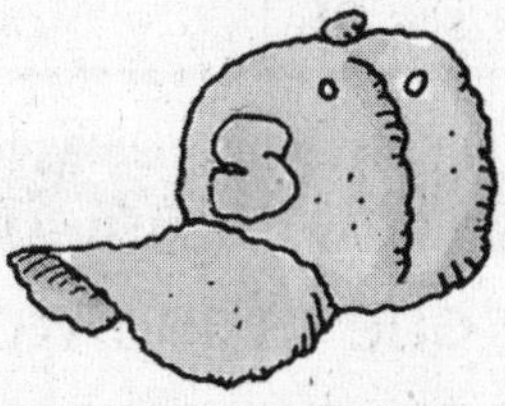

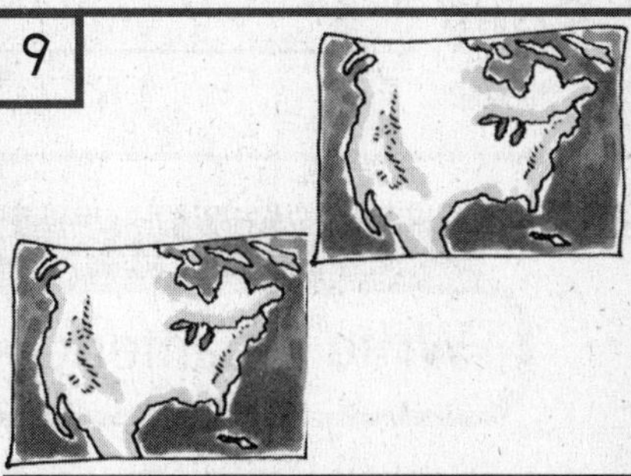

5

Name _____

Add **s** to each word to tell what each child does. Then trace the rest of the word. Read the sentences.

The cat looks.

1 Pam _____come_____ .

2 Jan _____pat_____ a cat.

3 Sam _____look_____ .

4 Dan _____tap_____ .

Write a sentence using one of the words above.

_____

_____

_____

Name _____

Circle the word that completes each sentence.
Then write the word.

1	_____ - - - - - - - - - - - - - - - - - - - I am a _____ .	cap cat
2	_____ - - - - - - - - - - - - - - - - - - - Here is a _____ .	map hat
3	_____ - - - - - - - - - - - - - - - - - - - The cat _____ .	sat taps
4	_____ - - - - - - - - - - - - - - - - - - - Here is a _____ .	pat mat
5	Look at _____ - - - - - - - - - - - - - - - - - - - that _____ !	ham cap

Name _____

Say the name of each picture. Write the word on the lines.

1		map
2		
3		
4		
5		
6		

Short Vowel: / a / a • Write Words

Phonics Practice Book

Name _____

Look at the picture. Read the sentence. Circle the word that completes the sentence. Then write the word.

1		_____ - - - - - - - - - - - I am _____ .	At Ann Add
2		_____ - - - - - - - - - - - Sam can _____ .	am dad add
3		_____ - - - - - - - - - - - This is _____ .	Add Matt Map
4		_____ - - - - - - - - - - - Can Pam _____ Dan?	pass jazz pan

Name _____

Look at each picture. Read the sentence. Use the letter sounds to read the words. Circle the word that completes the sentence. Then write the word.

#	Picture	Sentence	Words
1		Jan ran _____ .	fan fat fast
2		Max _____ Tab are cats.	and ant ask
3		We can _____ there.	cap camp cats
4		This is a _____ .	man map mask

Name _____

Look at the first picture in each row. Trace the picture name. Look at the other pictures and write the picture names. Then color the pictures.

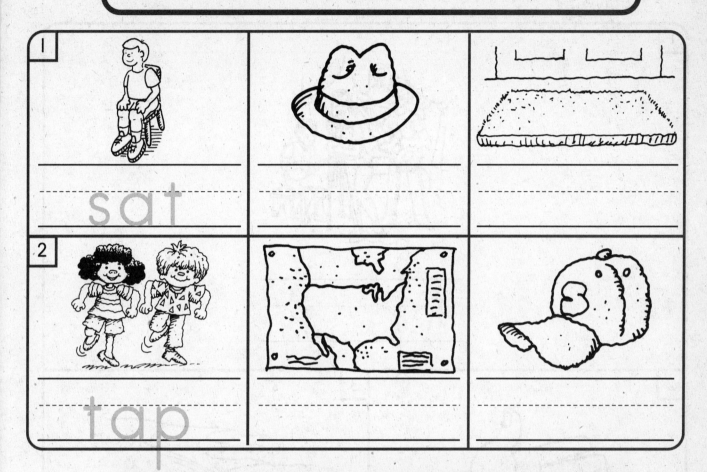

Read and trace the sentence. Then draw a picture about the sentence.

The cat sat in a hat.

© Harcourt

Name _____

1

band

2

_____

- - - - - - - - - - - - - - - -

_____

3

_____

- - - - - - - - - - - - - - - -

_____

© Harcourt

Name _____

Say the names of the pictures in each row. Color the pictures whose names rhyme and have the short **i** sound.

Name _____

Read each word. Color the picture it names.

1	**pit**	
2	**sip**	
3	**sit**	
4	**hit**	
5	**hid**	

Short Vowel: / i / i • Blending

Phonics Practice Book

© Harcourt

Name _____

Look at each picture. Write the word that completes the sentence.

| hit | pit | sip | hid | tip | sit |

1		Tim has a _____.
2		This is a big _____.
3		See Pam _____.
4		Come and _____ here.
5		See it _____!
6		The dog _____.

Write **a** or **i** to complete each picture name. Then trace the rest of the word.

1	2	3
h __ ll	c __ t	s __ p
4	5	6
p __ g	p __ t	c __ p
7	8	9
h __ t	m __ t	k __ ss
10	11	12
s __ d	d __ p	h __ d

© Harcourt

Read the sentences about each picture. Trace the contraction that stands for the underlined words.

1

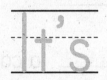

It + is = it's
It is a map.

It's a map.

2

He + is = he's
He is my dad.

He's my dad.

3

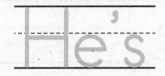

Here + is = here's
Here is my cat.

Here's my cat.

4

That + is = that's
That is a big hill.

That's a big hill.

Contraction: 's • Read and Write Words in Context

© Harcourt

Name _____

Look at each picture and read the first sentence.
Circle the contraction that stands for the two underlined
words. Then write it in the second sentence.

1		It is a cat. _____ - - - - - - - - - - - _____ a cat.	Sit It's I'ts
2		She is at bat. _____ - - - - - - - - - - - - - - - - - _____ at bat.	He's Sees She's
3		He is here. _____ - - - - - - - - - - - - - - - _____ here.	He's Hes H's
4		That is good! _____ - - - - - - - - - - - - - - - - - _____ good!	Thats Th'ats That's

Contraction: 's • Read and Write Words in Context

Phonics Practice Book

tack

Say the name of each picture. If it ends with the sound /k/, write **ck** on the lines.

1	2	3
ck		
4	5	6
7	8	9
10	11	12

Digraph: / k / *ck* • Phonemic Awareness

© Harcourt

Name _____

Read the word. Color the picture it names.

1			
tack			
2			
sick			
3			
kick			

Read the sentences. Use what you have learned about **ck** to read the underlined words. Then draw a picture to answer the question.

Here are <u>Jack</u> and <u>Rick</u>.
They have a <u>sack</u>.
What will they <u>pack</u> in the <u>sack</u>?

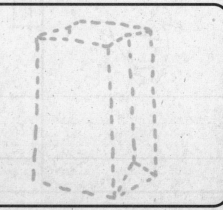

Digraph: / k / *ck* • Blending

Name _____

Write the word for each picture. The first word in each row can help.

1

lick _____   _____

2

sink _____   _____

Name _____

Write the word for each picture. The first word in each row can help.

1

pit _____ _____

2

Jill _____ _____

Phonograms: -it, -ill • Write Words

Phonics Practice Book

© Harcourt

Name _____

Color the pictures whose names have the short **o** vowel sound.

Short Vowel: / o / o • Phonemic Awareness

Name _____

Read each word. Color the picture it names.

1	**hot**	 	
2	**top**		
3	**cot**	 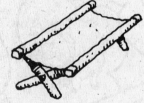	
4	**mop**	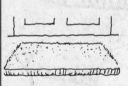 	
5	**pot**	 	

Short Vowel: /o/ o • Blending

Phonics Practice Book

Name _____

Look at each picture. Write the word from the box that completes the sentence.

hot   lock   hop   top   lot   cot

1 	_____ It can _____.
2 	_____ Don has a _____ of pots.
3 	_____ It is too _____.
4 	_____ Tom has a _____.
5 	_____ A cat is on the _____.
6	_____ I will _____ it.

© Harcourt

Name _____

Write **a, i,** or **o** to complete each picture name. Then trace the rest of the word.

1	2	3
c o t	c __ t	__ t p

4	5	6
c __ n	__ m p	s __ ck

7	8	9
h __ p	d __ ll	s __ ck

10	11	12
h __ t	p __ n	l __ ck

Short Vowels: / a / a, / i / i, / o / o • Review

Phonics Practice Book

Name _____

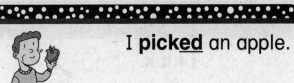

I **pick** an apple.   I **pick<u>ed</u>** an apple.

Add **ed** to each word to make a new word. Then trace the rest of the word. Read the new word.

1	2
fill	kick
3	4
land	look

Now write two sentences that use **ed** words.

_____

_____

_____

_____

© Harcourt

Name _____

I kick. **I am kicking.**

Add **ing** to each word to make a new word. Then trace the rest of the word. Read the new word.

1 pick

2 look

3 kiss

4 pack

Now write two sentences that use **ing** words.

_____

_____

_____

_____

Inflection: -ing • Write Words and Sentences   Phonics Practice Book

© Harcourt

Name _____

All the picture names end with **all**. Write the words.

1.

<u>ball</u>

2.

3.

4.

5.

6.

© Harcourt

Phonics Practice Book

Variant Vowel: / ô / a (all) • Write Words

29

Look at each picture and read the sentence. Circle the word that completes the sentence. Then write the word.

1	_____ I can kick the _____ .	bill ball bat
2	_____ Jan will _____ Kim.	call sill fall
3	_____ We _____ ran fast.	at ill all
4	_____ Will the man _____?	fall fill hall
5	_____ Let's sit on this_____ .	wig will wall
6	_____ This man is _____ .	till tall tack

Variant Vowel: / ô / a (all) • Read and Write Words in Context

Phonics Practice Book

© Harcourt

Look at each picture and read the sentence. Write the contraction that stands for the underlined words.

 can not = can't

 did not = didn't

 is not = isn't

 do not = don't

---

1

Dan <u>can not</u> see the big apple.

_____

Dan _____ see it.

2

Tom hid it, but <u>do not</u> look.

_____

Tom hid it, but _____ look.

3

Dan <u>did not</u> see it at all.

_____

Dan _____ see it at all.

4

Now the apple <u>is not</u> big.

_____

Now the apple _____ big.

Name _____

Color the block if the contraction stands for the two words below it.

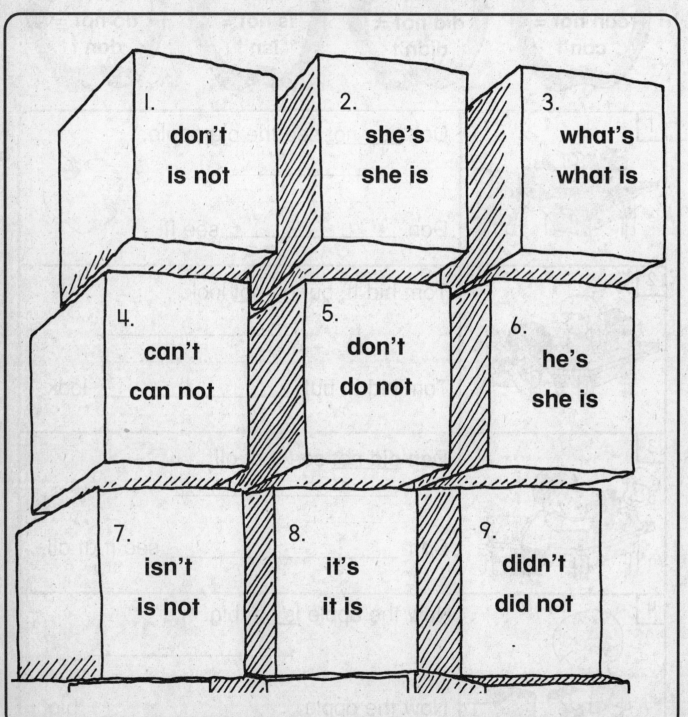

1. don't
is not

2. she's
she is

3. what's
what is

4. can't
can not

5. don't
do not

6. he's
she is

7. isn't
is not

8. it's
it is

9. didn't
did not

Say the name of each picture. Color the pictures whose names have the short **e** vowel sound.

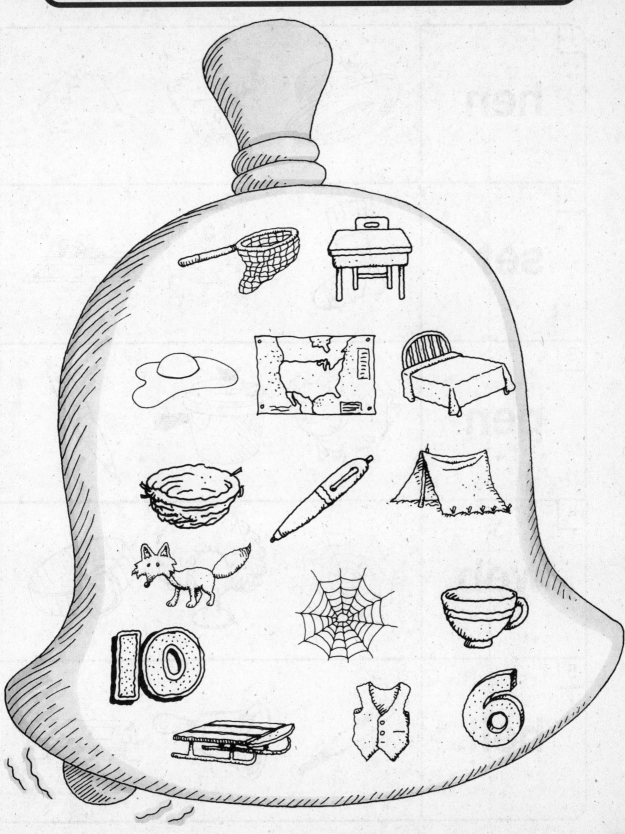

Read each word. Color the picture it names.

1	**hen**	
2	**set**	
3	**pen**	
4	**web**	
5	**bell**	

Short Vowel: / e / e • Blending

Phonics Practice Book

© Harcourt

Name _____

Look at each picture. Write the word from the box that completes the sentence.

hen   met   wet   fed   men   get

1

_____
She will _____ in.

2

_____
She _____ the dog.

3

_____
The _____ will go in.

4

Will the hen get
_____
_____ ?

5

_____
The _____
are not sad.

6

Sam has not
_____
_____ Ben.

Name _____

Write **o** or **e** to complete each picture name.
Then trace the rest of the word.

1	2	3	4
b__d	m__p	p__t	h__n
5	6	7	8
t__p	n__t	h__t	n__ck
9	10	11	12
c__t	h__p	b__ll	w__b

36 Short Vowels: / o / o, / e / e • Review

Phonics Practice Book

Say the name of the first picture in the row. Color the pictures whose names begin with the same two sounds.

Name _____

Write the two letters that complete each picture name.
Then trace the rest of the word.

bl   cl   fl   gl   pl   sl

1

_____
ap

2
_____
ag

3

_____
ant

4
_____
ock

5
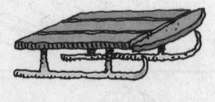
_____
ed

6

_____
ad

Initial Blends with l • Write Words   Phonics Practice Book

© Harcourt

Name _____

Say the name of each picture. Write **th** in the box that shows where you hear the sound in each word — at the beginning or at the end.

1	2	3
th	th	

4	5	6

7	8	9

Initial Digraph: / th / *th* • Phonemic Awareness

Name _____

Draw a line from the sentence to the picture it tells about.

1

This is a cat.

That is a dog.

2

This is thick.

That is thin.

Add the letter **t** to the picture names. Write and read the new words.

3

t +

_____

then

_____

4

t +

_____

_____

5

 + h

_____

_____

6

 + h

_____

_____

Name _____

1	_____ _____ _____ is your vest.	The This His
2	_____ _____ _____ you.	Think Tank Thank
3	My hat is _____ _____ _____ .	that thick tick
4	They play _____ _____ _____ me.	with win wink
5	Look at _____ _____ _____ jet.	then hat that

Draw a line from the sentence to the picture it tells about.

| 6 | This is big.

That is small. | 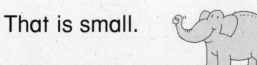 |
| 7 | This is a hat.

That is a map. |
 |

© Harcourt

Name _____

1 	Look at them! Come with me!
2 	Ed and Kim ran. Ed sits with Kim.
3 	"Thank you," said Beth. "Let's go," said Beth.
4 	Lad gets a bath. Lad got a big bat.
5 	I think I can add this. I see a big moth.
6 	Ann likes to pat the dog. Ann comes down the path.

Digraph: / th / *th* • Read Words in Context

© Harcourt

Say each picture name. Circle and write the letters that stand for the beginning sounds. Then trace the rest of the word.

1	sp (st) sm	stop
2	sl sn sk	ip
3	sn sl sc	ap

4	st sk sp	amp
5	sp sl sn	ip
6	sn sm st	all

7	st sp sn	in
8	sl st sn	ack
9	sk sl st	ick

10	sc sl sp	ot
11	sl sn st	ack
12	sk sp st	ill

Name _____

Circle the sentence that tells about the picture.

 **1**	Dan and Pam stand on the hill. Dan and Pam skip up the hill. Dan and Pam slid down the hill.
2	This hill is not small. This snack is too big. This stick will not snap!
 **3**	Dan and Pam pick up stamps. Dan and Pam snap a stick. Dan and Pam stop for a snack.
 **4**	Dan stands still. Dan spins a small top. Dan slips and spills it.
 **5**	Pam stops the spill. Pam sits still. Pam stands in a stall.

Name _____

Say the name of each picture. Color the pictures whose names have the short **u** vowel sound.

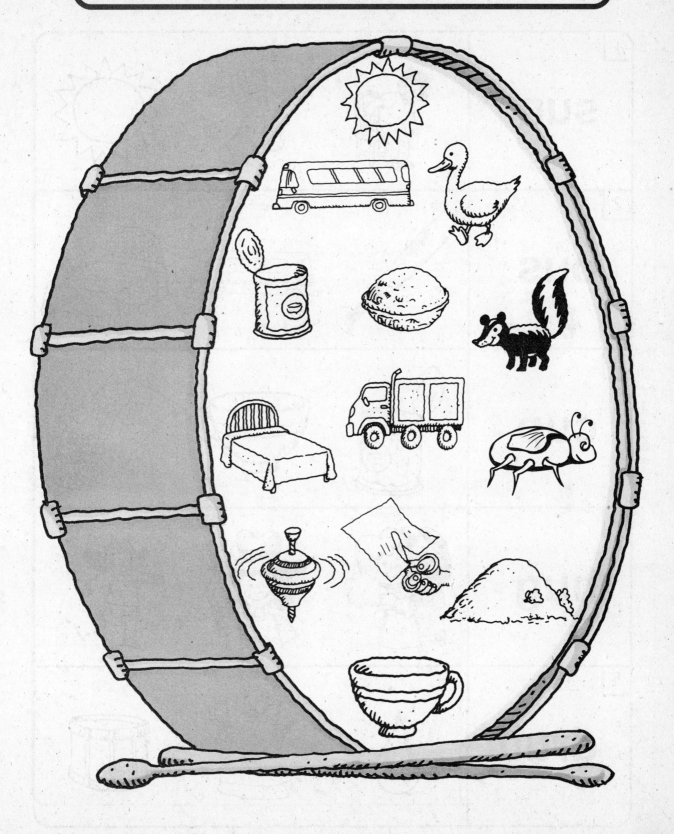

Short Vowel: / u / u • Phonemic Awareness

© Harcourt

Name _____

Read each word. Color the picture it names.

1	**sun**	 	
2	**bus**	 	
3	**cup**	 	
4	**hug**	 	
5	**drum**	 	

© Harcourt

Name _____

Write the name of each picture. Listen for the letter sounds to help you.

1	2	3
nut		

4	5	6

7	8	9

Short Vowel: / u / u • Write Words   47

Circle the sentence that tells about the picture.

#	Picture	Sentences
1		Ann likes the red cap. Ann picks up a cup. Ann is sick in bed.
2		The pot will get hot. The rug is red and tan. The can is not in the bag.
3		Let's mop up this mess. Let's mix this in a pan. Let's fill this big box.
4		Dad will fix the fan. Kim has a big black hat. Kim will fix it for Ron.
5		A pig went up a hill. A hen sits on a rock. A fox hops in a tub.
6		Ten cubs fit in the bed. The dog and pups got wet. Six cats nap in the sun.

Name _____

Say each picture name. Circle and write the letters that stand for the beginning sounds. Then trace the rest of the word.

1	fr (gr) tr	2	dr cr pr	3	fr cr tr
	grin		op		ack

4	gr fr tr	5	dr gr tr	6	dr fr tr
	ill		ip		ink

7	pr fr cr	8	dr pr cr	9	gr pr cr
	og		ill		ack

Initial Blends with *r* • Write Words

Name _____

1	Fran and Tramp go to the _____ _____.	track stack tack
2	Tramp sees a big _____ _____.	crack cap drink
3	Tramp is on the _____ _____.	grab grass drill
4	Fran sees a _____ _____.	crop prop drop
5	Now she sees a _____ _____.	grill rock frog

© Harcourt

Name _____

Read each word. Color the picture it names.

1	**king**	  
2	**bang**	 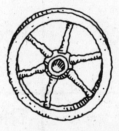 
3	**wing**	
4	**long**	
5	**ring**	 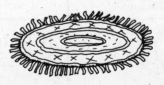 

© Harcourt

Name _____

Look at each picture. Write the word that completes the sentence.

| sting | long | rang | song | thing | bang |

1

Matt Cat sings a _____
_____ .

2

The bells _____ .

3

I can _____ you!

4

The glass fell with a
_____
_____ .

5

What is this
_____
_____ ?

6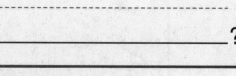

It is too
_____
_____ .

Name _____

Read the sentences about each picture. Write the
contraction that stands for the underlined words.

1 	**I + will = I'll** <u>I will</u> fix it for you. _____ ------------------------------- _____ fix it for you.
2 	**We + will = We'll** <u>We will</u> have fun! _____ ------------------------------- _____ have fun!
3 	**You + will = You'll** <u>You will</u> like my dog. _____ ------------------------------- _____ like my dog.
4	**They + will = They'll** <u>They will</u> have a snack. _____ ------------------------------- _____ have a snack.

Name _____

Look at each picture and read the sentence. Write the contraction that stands for the underlined words.

I will =
I'll

She will =
She'll

You will =
You'll

We will =
We'll

1		She will be glad we are here. _____ _____ be glad we are here.
2		I will help you pop it. _____ _____ help you pop it.
3		We will help you, too. _____ _____ help you, too.
4		You will eat it all! _____ _____ eat it all!

© Harcourt

Name _____

Color each picture whose name has the vowel sound /ôr/.

© Harcourt

Read each word. Color the picture it names.

1	**corn**	
2	**fork**	
3	**storm**	
4	**horn**	
5	**fort**	

© Harcourt

R-controlled Vowel: / ôr / or, ore • Blending

Phonics Practice Book

Name _____

Write the word that completes each sentence.

corn tore store storm thorn fort

1 	_____ This is a big _____.
2 	_____ This will be a good _____.
3 	_____ Oh, it's on a _____!
4 	_____ I _____ it!
5	_____ I got this at the _____.
6	_____ This is good _____.

© Harcourt

Name _____

The dog played a horn.
The cat got the corn.
The pig had a cork.
He forgot to get a fork!
The stork wore a hat.
Was there one more for the cat?

_____

1. The pig forgot a _____.

_____

2. The cat has the _____.

_____

3. The _____ wore a hat.

R-controlled vowel: / ôr / *or, ore* • Read and Write Words in Context   Phonics Practice Book

Name _____

Write the picture names. Use a word from the first box and a word from the second box to make each compound word.

bath   back   pop   sand   box   corn   tub   pack

1 _____
_____

2 _____
_____

3 _____
_____

4 _____
_____

Put the words together to make a compound word. Write the word to complete the sentence about the picture.

5
some + one

_____

There is _____ on the path.

6
some + thing

_____

Ted sees _____ red.

Name _____

1	This is a _____ windmill _____.	wingspan (windmill)
2	Tom's dog _____ _____ _____ go out.	checkup cannot
3	Let's go _____ _____ _____!	somewhere outfit
4	What is on the _____ _____ _____?	backpack desktop
5	They like to go _____ _____ _____.	upset downhill
6	_____ _____ That _____ looks good!	drumstick cockpit

Compound Words • Read and Write Words in Context

Phonics Practice Book

© Harcourt

Name _____

Color each picture whose name begins or ends with the sound /sh/.

Name _____

Read each word. Color the picture it names.

1			
ship			
2			
mash			
3			
shell	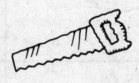		
4			
brush		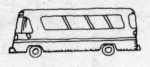	
5			
shelf			

Digraph: /sh/ *sh* • Blending

Phonics Practice Book

Name _____

Look at each picture. Write the word that completes the sentence.

flash   shelf   shop   rush   short   wish

1

_____

Meg will _____ for socks.

2

_____

What did Fred _____ for?

3

_____

This man is not _____!

4

_____

Jack and Beth have to _____.

5

_____

What will go on this _____?

6
_____

Look at that big _____!

Name _____

Write **th** or **sh** to complete each picture name.
Then trace the rest of the word.

1	2	3
di	mo	ba

4	5	6
in	pa	tra

7	8	9
ip	ink	fi

Digraphs: /th/ *th*, /sh/ *sh* • Review

Phonics Practice Book

Name _____

Circle the word that names the picture.

1.
tuck
truck
drum

2.
flap
slap
clap

3.
grin
spin
drip

4.
slick
click
stick

5.
slip
skip
grip

6.
drab
grab
crab

7.
flock
clock
crock

8.
skip
snip
clip

9.
track
crack
stack

10.
press
dress
fresh

11.
skill
spill
still

12.
plant
slant
grass

© Harcourt

Name _____

1	The _____ hops.	drag frog flop
2	Now it _____ .	swims trims spins
3	It stops for a _____ .	track stack snack
4	Come and play in the _____ .	glass grass class
5	It can still do a _____ .	trip drip flip
6	You need _____ to do this trick!	spill skill still

© Harcourt

Name _____

Color each picture whose name begins or ends with the sound /ch/.

1	2	3
4	5	6
7	8	9
10	11	12

© Harcourt

Say the name of each picture. Write **ch** if it begins with the sound for *ch.* Then trace the rest of the word.

1	2	3
_____ est	_____ ap	_____ eck

4	5	6
_____ ip	_____ op	_____ ing

7	8	9
_____ ick	_____ in	_____ ips

Digraph: / ch / ch • Write Words

Name _____

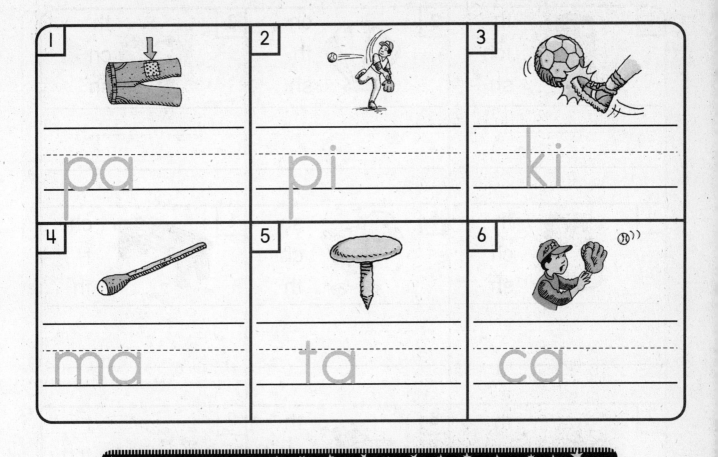

1. pa
2. pi
3. ki
4. ma
5. ta
6. ca

Say the name of each picture. Write **ch** if it ends with the sound for **ch**. Then trace the rest of the word.

7. ben
8. du
9. bran

Phonics Practice Book

Digraphs: / ch / ch, tch • Write Words

69

Name _____

Circle and write the letters that complete each picture name. Then trace the rest of the word.

1	th / tch / sh	pa__
2	ch / th / sh	__ell
3	th / ch / sh	__op
4	th / ch / sh	ba__
5	sh / ch / th	__ick
6	ch / t / th	ben__
7	th / ch / sh	fi__
8	th / ch / sh	__ip
9	t / tch / sh	ca__
10	sh / ch / h	__in
11	t / th / ch	bran__
12	th / sh / ch	__ick

Digraphs: /th/ th; /sh/ sh; /ch/ ch, tch • Review

Phonics Practice Book

Name _____

Add **es** to the words. Then use the words you wrote to complete the sentences.

glass

_____

_____

dish

_____

_____

wish

_____

_____

pass

_____

_____

_____

----

1. Ann put milk in the _____ .

_____

----

2. Ron got out the _____ .

_____

----

3. Ann _____ a dish to Ron.

_____

----

4. Tag _____ he had a snack, too.

Inflection: *-es* • Write Words

Add **es** to words that end with these letters: **x, ss, zz, sh, ch, tch**.

Write **es** to make each picture name tell about more than one. Then trace the rest of the word and read it.

1	2
_____ glass	_____ fox

3	4
_____ ash	_____ bench

Write the word that completes each sentence.

catches   kisses   buzzes

5	_____ Mom _____ him.
6	_____ He _____ it.
7	_____ It _____ .

Inflection: *-es* • Write Words   Phonics Practice Book

Color the pictures that have the vowel sound /är/.

© Harcourt

Name _____

1	**barn**	  
2	**park**	  
3	**star**	  
4	**cart**	  
5	**car**	  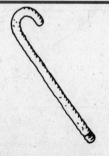

Write the name of each picture. Use the letter sounds
to help you.

1	2	3
bar		

4	5	6

7	8	9

R-controlled Vowel: / är / *ar* • Write Words

Name _____

Write the word that completes each sentence.

park   car   barn   card   hard   farm

1 	_____ It is _____ to find a pal like Mark.
2 	We went to the _____ _____ a lot.
3 	Now his home is on a _____ _____ .
4 	Mark likes to help in the _____ _____ .
5 	We will go there in the _____ _____ .
6 	For now, I will send a _____ _____ to Mark.

R-controlled Vowel: / är / *ar* • Read and Write Words in Context   Phonics Practice Book

© Harcourt

Circle and write the word that completes each sentence.

1	The cat _____ _____ with Ed's cap.	runs rung run
2	_____ Ed _____ for the cap.	looking look looked
3	_____ Pam _____ Ed.	calling call called
4	Pam was _____ _____ Ed's cap!	smash smashed smashing

© Harcourt

Name _____

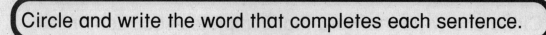

Circle and write the word that completes each sentence.

1	Did you see me _____ ‑‑‑‑‑‑‑‑‑‑‑‑‑‑‑‑‑‑‑‑‑‑‑‑‑‑‑‑‑ _____ it?	kicks kicking kicked
2	_____ ‑‑‑‑‑‑‑‑‑‑‑‑‑‑‑‑‑‑‑‑‑‑‑‑‑ Tim _____ them.	picking picks pick
3	Now Tim is _____ ‑‑‑‑‑‑‑‑‑‑‑‑‑‑‑‑‑‑‑‑‑‑‑‑‑‑‑‑ _____ them.	packs packed packing
4	_____ ‑‑‑‑‑‑‑‑‑‑‑‑‑‑‑‑‑‑‑‑‑ Pam was _____ for the cat.	look looking looks
5	_____ ‑‑‑‑‑‑‑‑‑‑‑‑‑‑‑‑‑ Then Pam _____ the cat.	calling calls called

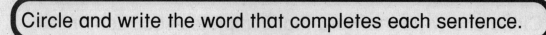

78

Inflections: -s, -ed, -ing • Read and Write Words in Context

Phonics Practice Book

© Harcourt

Name _____

Color each picture whose name begins with the sounds /kw/.

1	2	3
4	5	6
7	8	9

Quack!

© Harcourt

Color each picture whose name begins with the sound **wh**.

© Harcourt

Name _____

Look at each picture. Circle and write the word that completes the sentence.

1	Tom will mix and _____ _____.	whiz whip quack
2	_____ Kim can _____ the ball.	when quiz whack
3	I have lots of _____ _____.	quills quits whiffs
4	_____ Can you tell _____ one quacks?	quick wham which
5	_____ There is a _____ on the bed.	quilt quack when

© Harcourt

Circle the sentence that goes with each picture.

1 	This is when we have lunch. Let's quack like a duck. Did you pitch that in the trash?
2 	We quit dashing to the ship. We have to check the fish. We rush to catch the bus.
3 	They brush the dog's quilt. The dog gets a quick bath. The dog will have a quiz.
4 	This dish is for the chicks. The chicks are on a branch. They have a quilt for the fish.
5 	Quit quacking! They can quack! They are so quick!

© Harcourt

Double the final letter of most words with short vowels before adding **ed.**

Double the final consonant and add **ed** to each word. Then trace the rest of the word. Read the words.

 pop + p + ed = popped

1. hopped

2. pat

3. mop

4. tag

5. stop

6. skip

Name _____

Double the final consonant of most words with short vowels before adding **ing.**
Double the final consonant and add **ing** to each word. Then trace the rest of the word. Read the words.

 pop + p + ing = popping

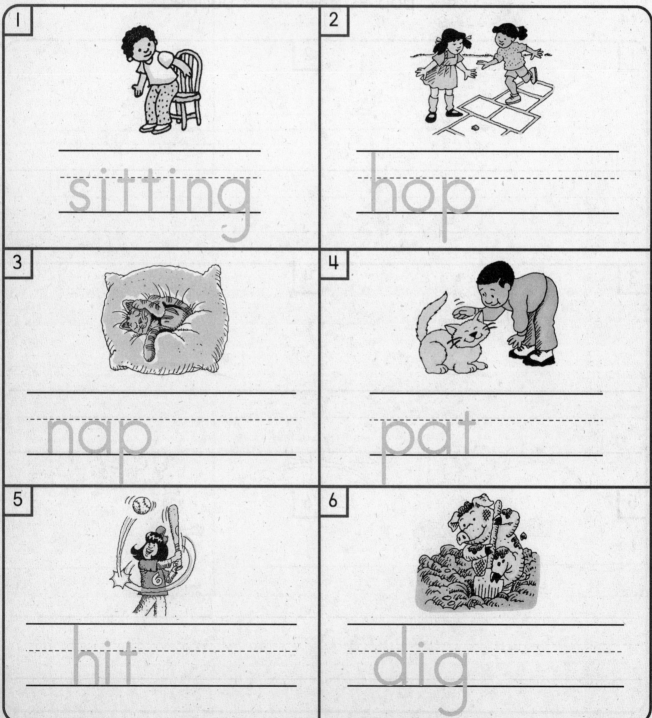

1 _____
   sitting

2 _____
   hop

3 _____
   nap

4 _____
   pat

5 _____
   hit

6 _____
   dig

Name _____

1	2	3
4	5	6
7	8	9

R-controlled Vowels: / ûr / *er, ir, ur* • Phonemic Awareness

Name _____

her

Write **er** to complete each picture name that has the vowel sound /ûr/. Then trace the rest of the word.

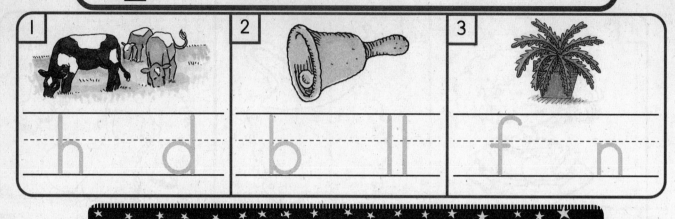

1. h __ d
2. b __ ll
3. f __ n

stir

Write **ir** to complete each picture name that has the vowel sound /ûr/. Then trace the rest of the word.

4. p __ g
5. b __ d
6. g __ l

curb

Write **ur** to complete each picture name that has the vowel sound /ûr/. Then trace the rest of the word.

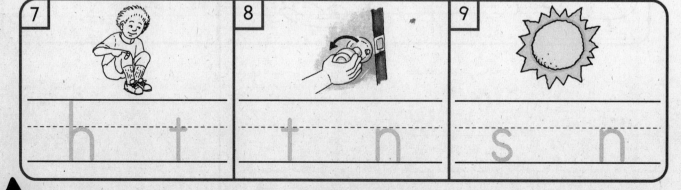

7. h __ t
8. t __ n
9. s __ n

R-controlled Vowels: / ûr / *er, ir, ur* • Write Words

Phonics Practice Book

© Harcourt

Name _____

Read each word. Color the picture it names.

1	hurt	  
2	bird	  
3	fern	 
4	shirt	  
5	turn	  

R-controlled Vowels: / ûr / *er, ir, ur* • Blending

Name _____

1	They find forks in a barn. They pick corn on a farm. They see cars next to the curb.
2	The dogs see a cart in the yard. The dogs start going north. The dogs bark at the stars.
3	This bird can see in the dark. This shirt got torn. The storm will start now.
4	The thorns are sharp. The bird has no horns. The first one has no fur.
5	Make a mark on the chart. Turn the short one now. Stir this with the fork.
6	The corks go back and forth. They perch in the ferns. They march as he plays a horn.

Add **er** to each word. Then trace the rest of the word.
Circle the one in each picture that the word tells about.

1 _____
fast

2 _____
sweet

Add **est** to each word. Then trace the rest of the word.
Circle the one in each picture that the word tells about.

3 _____
tall

4 _____
high

Inflections: -er, -est • Read and Write Words 89

Circle and write the word that completes each sentence.

#			
1		The truck is _____ than the car.	big biggest bigger
2		The truck parked in the back is _____ _____ .	taller tall tallest
3		That truck is the _____ _____ of them all.	fast fastest faster
4		Which car is the _____ _____ ?	older old oldest
5		_____ My car is _____ than your car.	smallest smaller small

Inflections: -er, -est • Read and Write Words in Context   Phonics Practice Book

Name _____

1	2	3
4	5	6
7	8	9
10	11	12

© Harcourt

Name _____

Write **le** to complete each word. Then draw a line from the word to the picture it names.

1	sadd _____	
2	pick _____	
3	kett _____	
4	app _____	
5	bott _____	

Syllable: / əl / -*le* • Write Words

Phonics Practice Book

© Harcourt

Name _____

CHUCKLES

My cat makes me giggle. So I call him Chuckles. When I pick Chuckles up, he will not wiggle or jiggle. He likes to cuddle and snuggle on my lap. As long as I have Chuckles, I will not grumble.

_____

1. Chuckles makes the girl _____.

_____

2. The cat likes to _____ and
_____

_____ .

_____

3. The girl will not _____ with Chuckles.

© Harcourt

Name _____

1	This man can _____ ------------------ _____ .	bubble tumble marble
2	The stars _____ ------------------ _____ .	purple candle sparkle
3	_____ ------------------ That _____ is hot!	handle saddle pickle
4	My belt has a big _____ ------------------ _____ .	buckle turtle bottle
5	The bells can _____ ------------------ _____ .	gobble jingle sample
6	Look at him _____ ------------------ _____ !	thimble juggle single

Syllable: / l / -le • Read and Write Words in Context.

Phonics Practice Book

© Harcourt

Name _____

Circle the word that completes the sentence. Then write the word.

1		
	_____ Dan _____ Tip.	part patted packed
2		
	_____ Tip _____ up on Dan.	hopped hop hopping
3		
	Dan _____ _____.	slipping slept slipped
4		
	Dan and Tip _____ _____ for a dip.	stopped stops stopping

Name _____

Read the rhyme. Then answer the question.

Go, Friends, Go!

Friends are nodding
and tapping.
Hands are snapping
and clapping.
Friends are spinning
and dipping.
Friends are tipping
and skipping.

We are hopping.
We are not stopping!

What are the friends doing?

_____

- -

_____

- -

_____

© Harcourt

Inflection: -ing (CVC) • Read and Write Words in Context   Phonics Practice Book

Name _____

Help the 🚣 go over the 〰️ . Color the pictures whose names have the long **o** vowel sound.

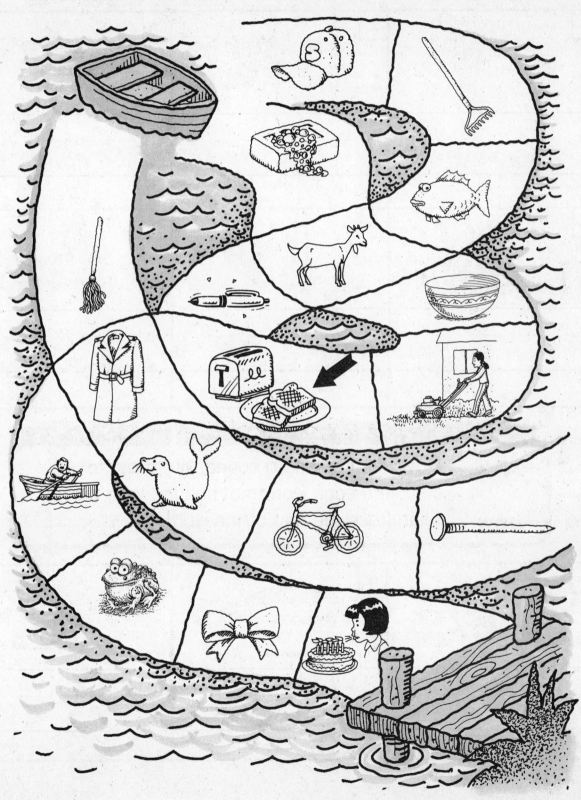

Long Vowel: /ō/ *ow, oa* • Phonemic Awareness

Boat has the long **o** sound. Write **oa** to complete each word that has the same sound. Then trace the rest of the word.

b<u>oa</u>t

1	2	3

___	___	___
coat	s___p	c___t
4	5	6
___	___	___
t___d	b___x	g___t

Bow has the long **o** sound. Write **ow** to complete each word that has the long **o** sound. Then trace the rest of the word.

b<u>ow</u>

7	8	9
___	___	___
sn___	p___t	b___l

© Harcourt

Name _____

1 **boat**

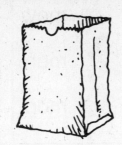  

2 **soap**

3 **coat**

4 **bowl**

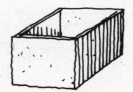  

5 **toad**

© Harcourt

Long Vowel: / ō / ow, oa • Blending

Circle the name of each picture. Then write the word.

1
got

get

goat

goat

2
mow

man

mop

3
sop

soap

sip

4
bell

box

bowl

5
cat

coat

cot

6
lad

load

log

7
rod

road

rose

8
snap

snow

sock

9
bet

bat

boat

© Harcourt

Name _____

Read the name of the first picture in each row. Write the other picture names.

1

boat _____   _____

2

snow _____   _____

3

load _____   _____

Name _____

Circle the word that completes each sentence. Then write the word.

1		_____ ------------------ Can he _____ them all out?	slow row blow
2		_____ ------------------ _____ us what you got from Joan.	Show Low Snow
3		Do you think they will _____ ------------------ _____ in the dark?	flow glow mow
4		How much have _____ ------------------ you _____?	thrown grown flown
5		_____ ------------------ What a big _____!	oat goat boat
6		I would like some _____ ------------------ _____.	boast toast coast

Name _____

Help the  get to the 🌳. Color the pictures whose names have the long **e** vowel sound.

Long Vowel: / ē / e, ee, ea • Phonemic Awareness

© Harcourt

Name _____

1	**peel**		 
2	**leaf**	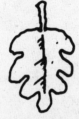	 
3	**feet**		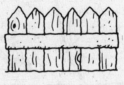 
4	**team**		 
5	**seal**	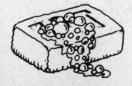	 

Long Vowel: / ē / e, ea, ee • Blending

Phonics Practice Book

© Harcourt

Name _____

Circle the name of each picture. Then write the word.

1			2			3		

1
bed
boat
bead

bead

2
seed
sell
sad

3
beak
best
back

4
pill
pet
peel

5
hen
he
heat

6
meal
melt
me

7
shed
sheep
ship

8
fast
felt
feet

9
road
read
rest

© Harcourt

Phonics Practice Book   Long Vowel: / ē / e, ea, ee • Read and Write Words   105

Name _____

Read the story. Then answer the question.

A DAY AT THE BEACH

One day we went to the beach. We saw that the beach was not clean. We all put the trash in green bags.

We had our meal near a big tree. Jean said that she saw a seal. Lee saw three bees.

Then it was time to go. But first we needed to make the beach clean and neat. Next week we will come back to this beach by the sea.

Why did they clean the beach?

_____

_____

_____

_____

Long Vowel: /ē/ e, ea, ee • Read and Write Words in Context   Phonics Practice Book

© Harcourt

Name _____

Read the sentences about each picture. Write the contraction that stands for the underlined words.

1

I + have = I've
<u>I have</u> had some milk.

_____

- - - - - - - - - - - - - - - -

_____ had some milk.

2

You + have = you've
<u>You have</u> run so fast!

_____

- -

_____ run so fast!

3

We + are = We're
<u>We are</u> going to have fun!

_____

- - - - - - - - - - - - - - - - - -

_____ going to have fun!

4

You + are = You're
<u>You are</u> a good dog.

_____

- - - - - - - - - - - - - - - - -

_____ a good dog.

© Harcourt

Name _____

Look at each picture and read the sentence. Write the contraction that stands for the underlined words.

I have =
I've

We have =
We've

They are =
They're

You are =
You're

1

We have played all day.

_____

_____ played all day.

2

You are hot.

_____

_____ hot.

3

I have had a rest now.

_____

_____ had a rest now.

4

They are going again.

_____

_____ going again.

Contraction: 've, 're • *Read and Write Words in Context*   Phonics Practice Book

Name _____

Help the 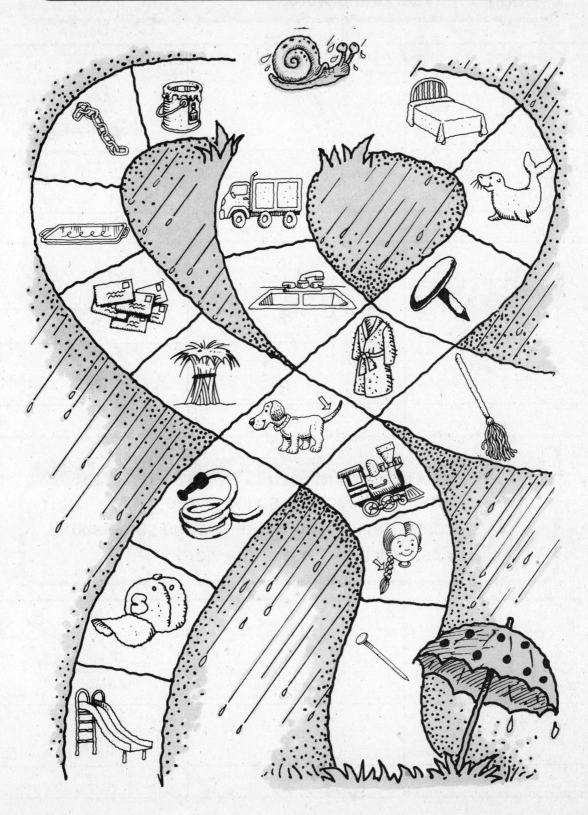 get out of the ///. Color the pictures whose names have the long **a** vowel sound.

Name _____

mail

Mail has the long **a** sound. Write **ai** to complete each word that has the same sound. Then trace the rest of the word.

1. p<u>ai</u>l

2. r _ _ n

3. v _ n

4. b _ t

5. p _ nt

6. sn _ l

jay

Jay has the long **a** sound. Write **ay** to complete each word that has the same sound. Then trace the rest of the word.

7. d _

8. pl _

9. p _ n

110

Long Vowel: /ā/ *ai, ay* • Write Words

Phonics Practice Book

© Harcourt

Circle the sentence that tells about the picture.

1. This is the day to play with Kay.
This is the way to Main Street.
This is the mail for Ray Green.

2. Gail has a braid.
Gail has a pain.
Gail has some clay.

3. Ray stays away.
Ray waits all day.
Ray pays for the nails.

4. The snail makes a trail.
The pail may sail away.
The chain is on a train.

5. Let's pay for this tray.
Let's play in this hay.
Let's paint this gray.

6. He may bring in the mail!
He got paint on his tail!
He put grain in his pail!

Name _____

Do what the sentences tell you to do. Then circle the words that have the long **a** sound.

1. Give the painter a pail of paint.

2. Find the tray. Color the plain cake on the tray.

3. Kay has braids and likes to play. Write **Kay** next to her.

4. Mrs. Day brings the mail. Write **Mrs. Day** next to her.

5. Jay has a boat. Put a sail on it.

6. Find the gray dog that waits. Put a tail on him.

Long Vowel: / ā / *ai, ay* • Read Words in Context

Phonics Practice Book

Name _____

Write the word for each picture. The first word in each row can help.

1

j<u>ay</u>

_____   _____

2

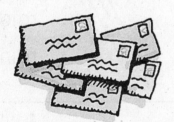  

m<u>ail</u>

_____   _____

3

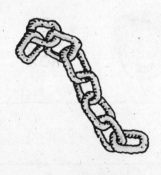  

ch<u>ain</u>

_____   _____

Name _____

1.
pan
pay
pail

pail

2.
chain
chin
cheap

_____

3.
hay
hat
hail

_____

4.
jam
jay
jeans

_____

5.
braid
branch
bray

_____

6.
rang
raid
rain

_____

7.
mail
main
meal

_____

8.
trap
trail
train

_____

9.
soap
say
sail

_____

Phonograms: -ay, -ain, -ail, -aid • Write Words

Phonics Practice Book

© Harcourt

Name _____

Say the names of the pictures in each row. Color two pictures whose names rhyme and have the long **a** sound.

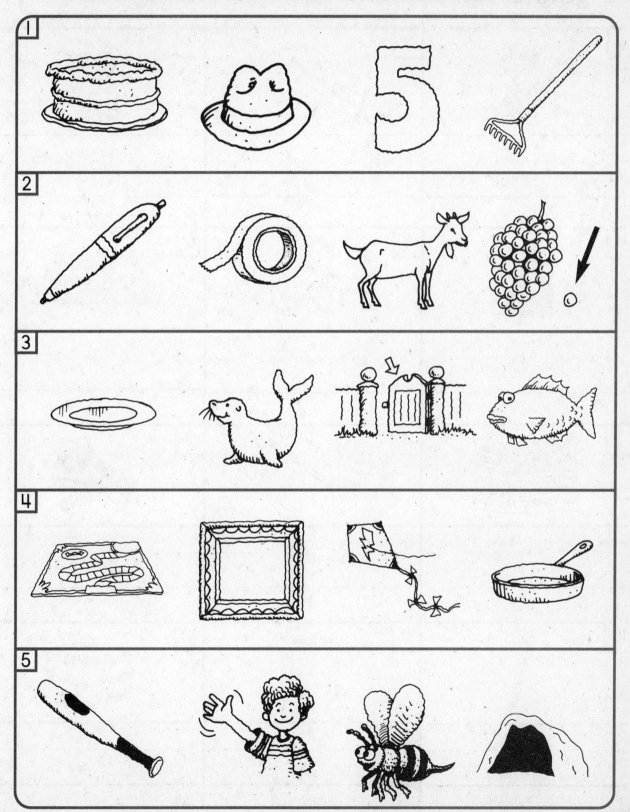

Phonics Practice Book

Long Vowel: / ā / a-e • Phonemic Awareness

115

Gate has the long **a** sound. Write **a** in the middle and **e** at the end of each word that has the same sound. Then trace the rest of the word. Read the words.

g**a**t**e**

1	2	3
w ___ v	t ___ p	c ___ t
4	5	6
c ___ n	sn ___ k	g ___ m
7	8	9
f l ___ g	r ___ k	s k ___ t
10	11	12
c ___ n	b ___ g	c ___ k

Long Vowel: /ā/ *a-e* • Write Words

Phonics Practice Book

© Harcourt

Circle the name of each picture. Then write the word.

1
rag
rack
(rake)

rake

2
gate
gape
got

_____

3
shave
shack
ship

_____

4
can
cane
coat

_____

5
tape
tap
top

_____

6
goat
gas
game

_____

7
grape
grab
grow

_____

8
snack
sneak
snake

_____

9
plane
plate
plot

_____

© Harcourt

Name _____

1 	We put on capes. We can't skate now. We are on a plane.
2 	We like to wade in the lake. We like to bake a cake. We like the same game.
3 	Jake adds his name. Jake waves to Kate. Jake shakes a cane.
4 	Kate reads a tale. Kate came in the gate. Kate gave Jake a frame.
5 	Jake is late for the game. Kate made a snake shape. Kate and Jake take some tape.
6	Kate and Jake ate cake. The grapes are on a plate. The plate is in a cave.

© Harcourt

Name _____

Write the word for each picture. The first word in each row can help.

1

snake

2

skate

3

plane

© Harcourt

Name _____

plate   trade   cake   lake

1

I can <u>bake</u> a _____ .

2

I <u>ate</u> everything on my

_____ .

3

I <u>made</u> a good _____ .

4

I like to <u>wade</u> in the

_____ .

© Harcourt

Say the names of the pictures in each row. Color the pictures whose names rhyme and have the long **i** sound.

Long Vowel: /ī/ *i-e* • Phonemic Awareness

nine

Nine has the long **i** sound. Write **i** in the middle and **e** at the end of each word that has the same sound. Then trace the rest of the word.

1 nine	2 r___k	3 h___v
4 p___n	5 v___n	6 d___v
7 k___t	8 b___k	9 g___m
10 h___t	11 f___v	12 l___n

© Harcourt

Name _____

Do what the sentences tell you to do.

1. Mike Miles rides a bike. Make a box around Mike Miles.

2. What is a mile up?  Color it.

3. Do you see a kite? Make it the same color as the vine.

4. Find the pile of pumpkins. Add one more to make nine.

5. Spike the cat likes to hide. Make a line under Spike. Put another cat by Spike's side.

Now circle the words that have the long **i** sound.

Name _____

1		A can or a cane?	
2		A bed or a bead?	
3		A kit or a kite?	
4		A cot or a coat?	
5		A pad or paid?	
6		Ran or rain?	
7		Rid or ride?	
8		A pin or a pine?	

Short and Long Vowels • Review

Phonics Practice Book

© Harcourt

When a word ends with **e**, drop the **e** before adding **ed**.
Write words that tell about the past. Drop the **e** and add
ed to each word.

chase – e + ed = chased

1	2	3
chase	**wave**	**close**
chased		

4	5	6
smile	**like**	**joke**

7	8	9
shave	**skate**	**trade**

© Harcourt

When a word ends with **e**, drop the **e** before adding **ing**.
Write new words. Drop the **e** and add **ing** to each word.

chase – e + ing = chasing

1	2	3
chase	**trade**	**ride**
chasing		

4	5	6
wave	**joke**	**come**
	Knock, knock. Who's there?	

7	8	9
shave	**close**	**give**

© Harcourt

Name _____

 Rope has the long **o** sound. Write **o** in the middle and **e** at the end of each word that has the same sound. Then trace the rest of the word.

r͟o͟p͟e͟

1	2	3
r ___ p ___	b ___ n ___	m ___ p ___

4	5	6
p ___ l ___	p ___ t ___	r ___ s ___

7	8	9
t ___ p ___	r ___ b ___	c ___ n ___

10	11	12
n ___ s ___	b ___ x ___	h ___ l ___

© Harcourt

Name _____

1

nod
nest
(nose)

nose

2

rope
rock
row

_____

3

meal
mole
mop

_____

4

not
net
note

_____

5

can
cone
cane

_____

6

rob
robe
rub

_____

7

rods
road
rose

_____

8

pal
pole
pill

_____

9

bean
bun
bone

_____

Name _____

hose	bone	joke
mole	hope	hole

_____

1. I have a big _____ .

2. I will put it in this _____ .

3. Joan went to get the _____ .

4. I _____ she did not see me.

5. I'll say a _____ did it.

6. Will she smile at my _____ ?

© Harcourt

Name _____

Write the word that names each picture.

goat   rope   kite   cake   hole   hay
train   bowl   tree   cone   leaf   rose

1	2 	3 
_____	_____	_____
4 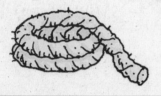	5 	6 
_____	_____	_____
7 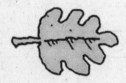	8	9
_____	_____	_____
10 	11 	12 
_____	_____	_____

Long Vowels • Review   Phonics Practice Book

Name _____

Write the word for each picture. The first word in each row can help.

1

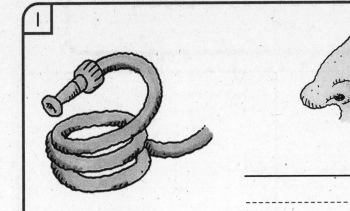 

h<u>ose</u>

_____   _____

2

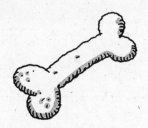  

b<u>one</u>

_____   _____

3

m<u>ole</u>

_____   _____

Name _____

Read the sentence pairs. Use the underlined word in the first sentence to think of a word to complete the second sentence. Write the word. Then draw a picture about the sentence.

1 I saw a <u>mole</u>. _____ - - - - - - - - - - - - - - - It peeked out of its _____.	
2 Bob and I spoke. _____ - - - - - - - - - - - - - - - - I was telling him a _____.	
3 I started to poke it. _____ - - - - - - - - - - - - - - - - Then I _____ it.	
4 I sniff at the rose. _____ - - - - - - - - - - - - - - - - It tickles my _____.	

© Harcourt

Write **c** to complete each word. Read the word and draw a line to the picture it names.

1	_____ircus	
2	_____ircle	
3	_____enter	

Write **ce** to complete each word. Read the word and draw a line to the picture it names.

1	ra_____	
2	fen_____	
3	mi_____	

Name _____

Write **g** to complete each word. Read the word and draw a line to the picture it names.

1	_____em_____	
2	_____entle_____	
3	_____erbil_____	

Write **dge** to complete each word. Read the word and draw a line to the picture it names.

1	ba_____	
2	bri_____	
3	we_____	

© Harcourt

134

Consonants: / j / g, *dge* • Read and Write Words

Phonics Practice Book

Write **c** or **g** to complete the picture name. Then trace the rest of the word. Read the words.

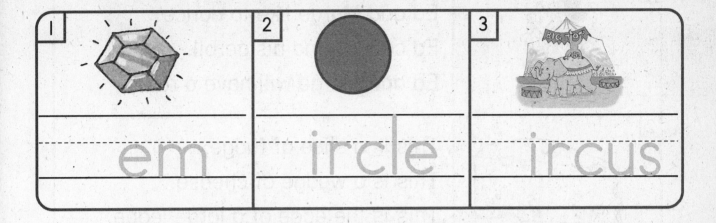

1	2	3
__em	__ircle	__ircus

Write the letter that completes the picture name. Then trace the rest of the word.

4	5	6
brid__e	__edge	dan__e

7	8	9
ra__e	mi__e	sta__e

Consonants: / s / c; / j / g, dge • Write Words

Name _____

1.
   Ed and Marge like to dance.
   Ed cannot find his gerbil.
   Ed and Marge will have a race.

2.
   This is a slice of fudge.
   This is a wedge of cheese.
   This is the edge of a large ledge.

3.
   What is the price of this bag?
   What is the bridge doing here?
   Where is the shopping center?

4.
   Madge will not dance with the prince.
   Madge and I went to the circus twice.
   Madge and Midge are such nice mice.

5.
   The bridge is a place to prance.
   The bridge goes across a river.
   The bridge goes across a ledge.

6. Do this to ice a large cake.
   Do this to get a badge.
   Do this to get rid of germs.

Circle and write the contraction that completes each sentence.

#			
1		_____ _____ get this for my bird.	I'm I'll I've
2		_____ It _____ cost much.	doesn't they'll weren't
3		_____ _____ our turn next.	Isn't It's I'm
4		_____ _____ add up our bill.	Hasn't He's He'll
5		_____ It _____ too big to fit.	haven't wasn't you'll
6		_____ _____ go home.	Didn't Let's Can't

Color the hat if the contraction stands for the two words below it.

1	2	3
I'm / I am	wasn't / will not	they'll / they will
4	5	6
I'll / I will	it's / it is	weren't / were not
7	8	9
she's / she will	can't / can not	he'll / he will
10	11	12
didn't / is not	let's / let us	you'll / you will

© Harcourt

Name _____

Find the long **u** words in the puzzle. Circle them. Some words go across. Some words go down.

mule	cute	huge	cube

c	u	b	e	m
u	l	r	w	h
t	f	s	o	u
e	d	t	k	g
z	m	u	l	e

Now write the word that goes with the picture.

1. _____

2. _____

3. _____

4. _____

Name _____

huge	use	cute
mule	cube	

_____

1. The _____ is in the garden.

_____

2. Luke will _____ his cap to chase it out.

_____

3. The ducklings are _____.

_____

4. One duckling thinks the horse is _____.

_____

5. Mom puts an ice _____ in the pitcher.

Long Vowel: / (y)o͞o / u-e • Read and Write Words

Phonics Practice Book

© Harcourt

★ ★ ★ ★ ★ ★ ★ ★ ★ ★ ★ ★ ★ ★

Read and write each word. Add an **e** to the end to make a word with a long vowel sound. Draw a picture for each new word.

1 tub	_____ - - - - - - - - - - - _____	
2 can	_____ - - - - - - - - - - - _____	
3 cut	_____ - - - - - - - - - - - _____	
4 rob	_____ - - - - - - - - - - - _____	
5 pin	_____ - - - - - - - - - - - _____	
6 cub	_____ - - - - - - - - - - - _____	

© Harcourt

Name _____

1	Dave shows her a goat. Jake eats his meal. Mike will take the mail.
2	A snake meets a snail. A seal dreams of the sea. A cute snail eats a cake.
3	The jay sees a kite. He plays with the flute. He has a seed in his beak.
4	The dog eats ice cubes. The dog's bone floats away. The dog's nose is yellow.
5	Look what the mule uses to see! The mule can play a tune! A mule gets sweet green grapes.
6	Rose paints a gate gray. Joan uses soap on the sheep. Kate makes a goat from clay.

© Harcourt

Drop the final **e**, and add **ed** to the words below to make new words. Read the words.

move
_____
- -

hope
_____
- -

_____

surprise
_____
- -

_____

dance
_____
- -

_____

Now use the words you wrote to complete the story.

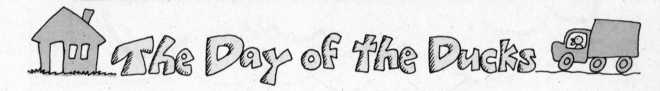

The Day of the Ducks

_____
- -

1. One day some ducks _____ into a house.

_____
- -

2. That _____ me!

_____
- -

3. Three little ducks _____ together.

_____
- -

4. I _____ we could all be friends.

Name _____

Drop the final **e**, and add **ing** to the words below. Then use the words you wrote to complete the sentences.

dance

_____

ride

_____

come

_____

chase

_____

_____

1. Look! My book friends are _____ out.

_____

2. One is _____ a horse.

_____

3. One is _____ her sheep.

_____

4. One is _____ with a mouse.

© Harcourt

Name _____

1 **cry**			
2 **tie**			
3 **sky**			
4 **fry**			

© Harcourt

Name _____

The **y** in **shy** and the **ie** in **lie** both stand for the long **i** sound. Write the word that completes each sentence.

sh<u>y</u>

l<u>ie</u>

| tie | fly | pie | try | sky |

_____

1. Birds can _____.

_____

2. They go up in the _____.

_____

3. I'll _____ these wings to my shell.

_____

4. Then I'll give it a _____.

_____

5. Oh my! Don't cry. Have some _____.

Long Vowel: /ī/ y, ie • Read and Write Words in Context

Phonics Practice Book

© Harcourt

Name _____

The **igh** in **right** stands for the long **i** sound. Write the word that completes each sentence.

right

| light | high | night | fright | bright |

_____

1. One _____ I woke up.

_____

2. I saw a _____ in the sky.

_____

3. The light was very _____.

_____

4. It gave me a _____.

_____

5. It was a plane _____ up in the sky!

Name _____

Circle the name of each picture. Then write the word.

1

sip
sea
(sigh)

sigh

2

light
list
lie

_____

3

frog
fright
fry

_____

4

bring
bite
bright

_____

5

high
hug
hide

_____

6

tag
tight
tie

_____

7

ring
right
ride

_____

8

nine
nest
night

_____

9

flight
flip
float

_____

© Harcourt

Long Vowel: /ī/ *igh* • Read and Write Words

Name _____

Look at each picture, and read the sentence. Write the contraction that stands for the underlined words.

I would = I'd   they would = they'd
we have = we've   you are = you're

1

<u>You are</u> not going to sit down, are you?

_____

_____ not going

to sit down, are you?

2

Yes, <u>we have</u> danced all night.

_____

Yes, _____ danced all night.

3

But <u>I would</u> like to dance more.

_____

But _____ like to dance more.

4

I wish <u>they would</u> dance with me!

_____

I wish _____ dance

with me!

Name _____

1. This tree <u>isn't</u> very big.	is not can not
2. <u>We're</u> going to plant it here.	We have We are
3. <u>You've</u> found a good place.	You have They have
4. It <u>couldn't</u> be better.	could not did not
5. <u>She'll</u> get some water for it.	She is She will
6. <u>I'd</u> like to help, too.	I would He would
7. <u>It's</u> fun to plant a little tree!	It will It is

© Harcourt

Name_____

Write **ow** if the picture name has the vowel sound /ou/. Then trace the rest of the word.

owl

1. c____

2. cl____n

3. f____ld

4. cr____d

5. b____

6. t____st

7. cr____n

8. t____n

Vowel Diphthong: / ou / *ow* • Write Words

© Harcourt

Name _____

Circle and write the word that completes the sentence.

1	We like to get out and go to _____ ------------------------------ _____ .	team town ten
2	We look around. Why is there a _____ ------------------------------ _____?	crown crate crowd
3	"Look!" I shout. "It's a _____ ------------------------------ _____!"	clean clown clam
4	_____ ------------------------------ I found out _____ he jumps so high.	how howl home
5	We shout out loud and he takes _____ ------------------------------ a _____ .	brown bow down

Now go back and read the sentences. Circle and say the words with **ou.**

152

Vowel Diphthong: / ou / *ow, ou* • Read and Write Words in Context   Phonics Practice Book

© Harcourt

Name_____

1 now

2 c

3 b

4 w

Add letters to the beginning of **out** to make new words. Write the words. Draw a picture for each new word.

5 out

6 sh

7 p

8 sc

© Harcourt

Name _____

Change the first letter in **down** to make new words.
Write the words. Draw a picture for each new word.

1	2
down	t
3	4
cl	br

Change the first letter in **found** to make new words.
Write the words. Draw a picture for each new word.

5	6
found	gr
7	8
s	r

Phonograms: *-own, -ound* • Write Words

Phonics Practice Book

154

© Harcourt

Name _____

The **y** in **puppy** and the **ie** in **puppies** both stand for the long **e** sound. Write the word that completes each sentence.

puppy

puppies

| field | sunny | bunny | happy | bunnies |

_____

1. Billy the _____ looked outside.

_____

2. It was _____ out.

_____

3. He called all the _____.

_____

4. Now they are all in the _____.

_____

5. They are _____ bunnies.

Name _____

Circle the name of each picture. Then write the word.

1

happen
happy
hopping

_____

- - - - - - - - - - - - - - - -

_____

2

field
filled
felt

_____

- - - - - - - - - - - - - - - -

_____

3

puppets
pumps
puppies

_____

- - - - - - - - - - - - - - - -

_____

4

supper
sudden
sunny

_____

- - - - - - - - - - - - - - - -

_____

5

snort
sneak
snowy

_____

- - - - - - - - - - - - - - - -

_____

6

pens
ponds
pennies

_____

- - - - - - - - - - - - - - - -

_____

7

chief
chain
chill

_____

- - - - - - - - - - - - - - - -

_____

8

mutter
muddy
muddle

_____

- - - - - - - - - - - - - - - -

_____

9

chilly
chicks
chuckle

_____

- - - - - - - - - - - - - - - -

_____

© Harcourt

Long Vowel: / ē / y, ie • Read and Write Words

Phonics Practice Book

Name _____

Draw lines to show which words go together.

1		2		3	
Words About the Sky		**Words About an Animal**		**Words About a Field**	
sun	starry	fur	jumpy	grass	lumpy
cloud	sunny	jump	puppy	rock	grassy
star	cloudy	pup	furry	lump	rocky

Now draw a picture. Show the sky and an animal in a field. Draw yourself in the picture, too. Then circle the words in the boxes above that tell about your picture.

Long Vowel: / ē / y, ie • Read Words

Name _____

A Silly Story

Bobby Dog and his buddy hurry into the city.
Bobby's pal is a seal, and her name is Kitty!

They see Donny Duck and a pig named Bunny.
Bunny put on a wig and looks ever so funny!

Do you think this story is much too silly?
Well, I can tell you another about a bunny named Tillie!

_____

- -

1. Bobby and Kitty hurry into the _____ .

_____

- -

2. The duck's name is _____ .

_____

- -

3. The pig's name is _____ .

© Harcourt

Add **es** to some words to tell about more than one. If a word ends with **y**, change the **y** to **i** before adding **es**. Look at the word that tells about one. Change the **y** to **i** and add **es** to write a word that tells about more than one.

1 family

families

2 baby

Add **es** to some words that tell about now. If a word ends with **y**, change the **y** to **i** before adding **es**.

Look at the word that tells about now. Change the **y** to **i** and add **es** to write a word that tells about now.

3 They fly.

It _____.

4 They try.

He _____.

Name _____

Read and trace the first word. Add **er** and **est** to make
new words. Don't forget to change the **y** to **i** before you
add the endings.

1		
happy	happier	happiest

2		
sunny	sunn___	sunn___

3		
silly	sill___	sill___

4		
snowy	snow___	snow___

Inflections: *-er, -est* (Change *y* to *i*) • Read and Write Words
Phonics Practice Book

© Harcourt

Name _____

Circle the word that names the picture. Then write the word.

1	boot boat ball	2	toast tot tooth	3	no new now

boot

4	chew check chop	5	hoot hot hall	6	brick broke broom

7	flow flew float	8	soon spin spoon	9	moon moan man

10	got goose goat	11	blur boost blew	12	threw toot throne

Circle the sentence that tells about the picture.

1.
Let's sit in the boat.

Let's get some new boots.

Let's sit in the booth.

2.
Look at that big moon!

Look at that big moose!

Look at the bright sun!

3.
I will get a few apples.

I will get a new bag.

I like this new coat.

4.
Lewis scoops it up with a fork.

Lewis will get home soon.

Lewis mixes it with a spoon.

5.
My pet bird likes this food.

My pet bird sleeps in a boot.

My pet is a big, tall moose.

6.
All the birds perched in the tree.

All the birds flew away.

All the birds swam in the pond.

Vowel Diphthong: / o͞o / oo, ew • Read Words in Context   Phonics Practice Book

Name _____

Complete each group of sentences. Write words that end with **ool** and **ew**.

1

He is not _cool_.

2

It is not _new_.

3

This is a _____.

4

The wind _____.

5

Sit on the _____.

6

Look what I _____.

7

Swim in the _____.

8

The birds _____.

Phonograms: *-ool, -ew* • Write Words

Name _____

Circle the sentence that tells about each picture.

1		We'd hop if we could. I'd like you to hop in. You're hopping away.
2		We're playing a game. They've been swimming. You're a good dancer.
3		You're not going to find the bag. We'd better get up now. He'd packed his lunch in the bag.
4		They're going to hop back in the pot! We've seen a pot hop! They've popped out of the pot!
5		I've dropped the can. You're making a big mess. I'd like something to drink.
6		You've come to a hot place. You're a good skater. You'd be cold in this place.

© Harcourt

Contractions: 'd, 've, 're • Read Words in Context

Phonics Practice Book

Name _____

The **i** in **hi** stands for the long **i** sound. Write the word that completes each sentence.

hi̲

find   child   I   grind   kind

_____
- -

1. "Who will help me _____ this wheat?"

_____ "
- - - - - - - - - - - - - - - - - - - -

2. "Not _____, said the pig.

_____
- -

3. Can the hen _____ some help?

_____
- -

4. A _____ helps the hen.

_____ "
- -

5. "You are very _____, says the hen.

© Harcourt

Write the word that completes each sentence.

| find | I | wild | kind | behind |

1

My cat Spike

_____

- -

is a little bit _____.

2

He likes to hide

_____

- -

_____ things.

3

Other cats always

_____

- - - - - - - - - - - - - - - - - - -

_____ him!

4

_____

- -

One time, _____

saw that Spike was sick.

5

The vet was

_____

- - - - - - - - - - - - - - - - - - -

very _____ to him.

Long Vowel: / ī / i • Read and Write Words in Context

Phonics Practice Book

Old has the long **o** sound. Write **o** to complete each word that has the same sound. Then trace the rest of the word.

old

1.

old

2.

pple

3.

c ld

4.

n

5.

f ld

6.

f x

7.

k te

8.

s ld

9.

g ld

Name _____

1		_____ - - - - - - - - - - - - - - - - Can we _____ for a swim?	got go game
2		_____ - - - - - - - - - - - - - - I will _____ mine.	feed fog fold
3		_____ - - - - - - - - - - - - - I like to _____ it up.	roll rock rail
4		_____ - - - - - - - - - - - - - The water is _____.	cot cost cold
5		_____ - - - - - - - - - - - - - Now _____ of us are warm!	box both bay

Long Vowel: /ō/ o • Read and Write Words in Context

Phonics Practice Book

© Harcourt

Name _____

Read and write the words in the box.

find	hold	wild	kind	told	wind	fold
cold	child	mind	grind	gold	mild	rind	sold

1 **Words that End with _ind_**

find

2 **Words that End with _old_**

hold

3 **Words that End with _ild_**

wild

CUT-OUT FOLD-UP BOOKS

Where is Pat?

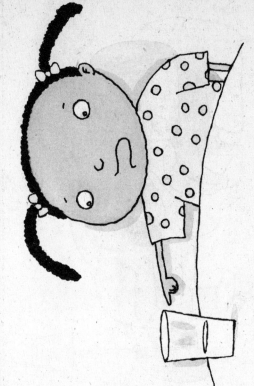

Did Pat sit here?

Did Pat sip this?

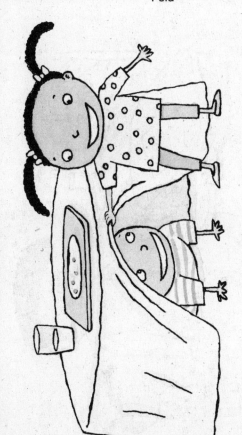

Pat is here!

Pat hid.

Did Pat come here?

Pat? Pat?

8

6

2

Is Pat here?

Where is Pat?

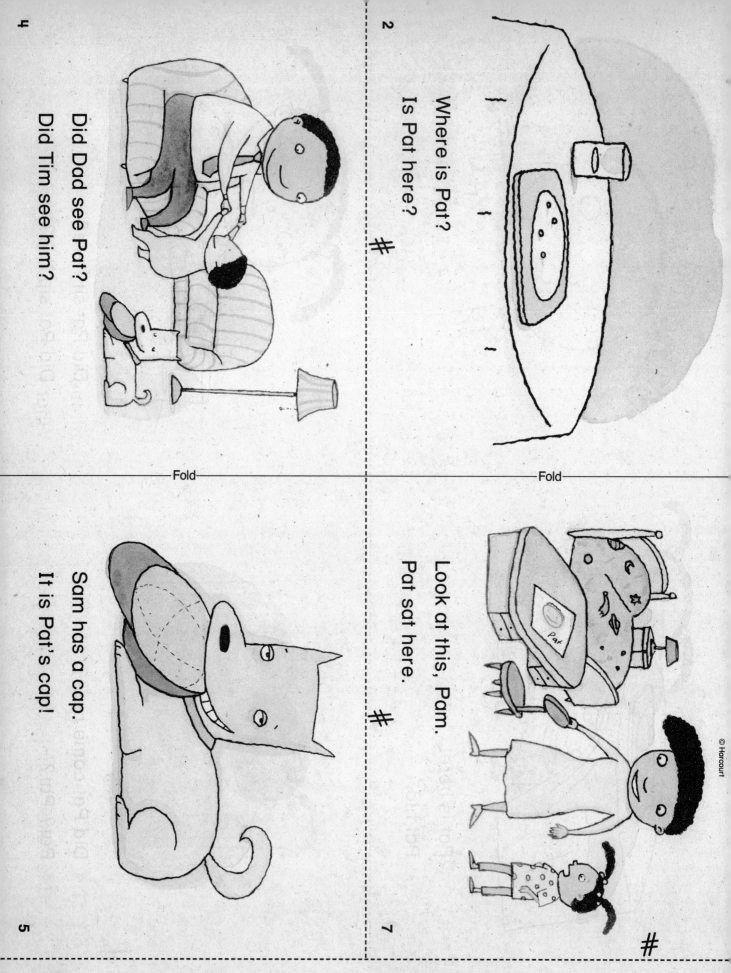

#

Did Dad see Pat?
Did Tim see him?

Fold

Fold

Pat sat here.

Look at this, Pam.

#

Sam has a cap.
It is Pat's cap!

© Harcourt

#

Cut-Out, Fold-Up Book 1 • Review

Directions: Help your child cut out and fold the book.

KIDS ON THE GO!

1

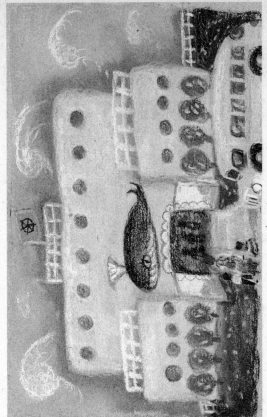

All the kids go in.
What will the kids see?

3

Thank you!
We will come back soon.

8

This isn't a pond.
It is called a tank.

6

All the kids get maps.
They will not get lost.

All the kids hop in.
Off they will go!

Fold

Fold

That is big!
It's as big as a wall!

It will pass and dip, pass and dip.
All the kids like it a lot!

© Harcourt

Cut-Out, Fold-Up Book 2 · Review

Directions: Help your child cut out and fold the book.

A Pet for Buzz Bug

— Fold —

A hen will sit for a long, long time.

— Fold —

Rocks do not run or eat bugs. "A rock is the best pet for me!" said Buzz Bug.

8

A frog sits on a pad and eats bugs. A frog is not a good pet for a bug!

6

2

Buzz Bug wants a big pet. "What if I get a pet hen?" asked Buzz Bug.

—Fold—

4

A duck swims on a pond. It will swish and swim. It's not fun for a bug to swish and swim.

—Fold—

7

Buzz Bug rests on a rock in the sun. Rocks do not sit on eggs or swish and swim.

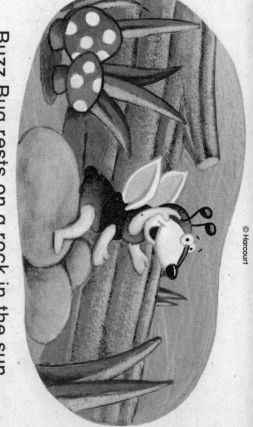

© Harcourt

5

A fox runs on the grass. A bug does not like to run fast like a fox.

Cut-Out, Fold-Up Book 3 · Review

Directions: Help your child cut out and fold the book.

Barb and the Corn

"Corn helps little birds grow," thinks Barb. "I will get a bunch of chicks!"

Fold

3

Fold

Barb still has lots of corn left. "Do turtles like corn?" she thinks.

8

The little birds chirp and chirp. "Quit it!" Barb tells them, but they aren't stopping.

6

© Harcourt

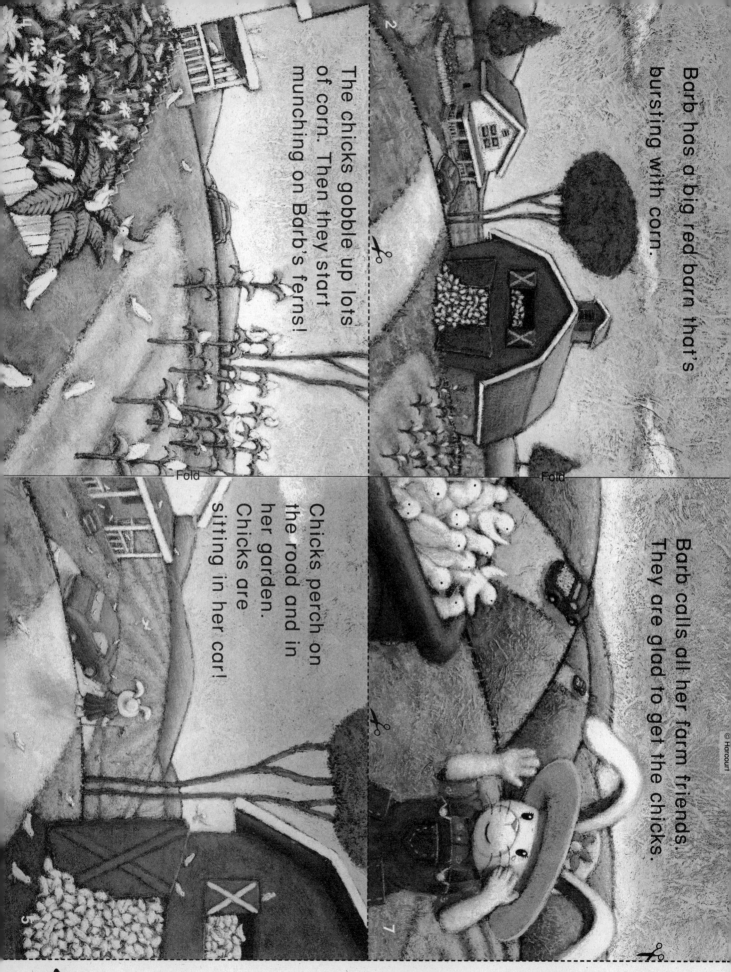

Barb has a big red barn that's bursting with corn.

The chicks gobble up lots of corn. Then they start munching on Barb's ferns!

Barb calls all her farm friends. They are glad to get the chicks.

Chicks perch on the road and in her garden. Chicks are sitting in her car!

Fold

Fold

© Harcourt

Directions: Help your child cut out and fold the book.

TIME TO DREAM

1

3

The sun sets at the end of the day.
The birds in the trees see the sun's last ray.

Fold

Fold

© Harcourt

Snuggle in as the stars glow and gleam.
It's time to sleep. It's time to dream.

8

It's time to make the last catch of the day.
Then we skip home. We can't stay and play.

6

2

Hens cluck and chicks cheep.
It's time to go home. It's time to sleep.

4

Rabbits eat sweet, green grass at the edge
of the park. Then they race to their hole
when it begins to get dark.

7

The sun will go down without a trace,
while we're all snug in a nice safe place.

5

Frogs plunge into the lake for one
last swim, before the sun fades and
it begins to get dim.

Fold

Fold

© Harcourt

⭐ 180   Cut-Out, Fold-Up Book 5 • Review

Directions: Help your child cut out and fold the book.

Jo and June

They raced over the field and down the trail. They were soon at the pond to see a boat sail.

Fold

It was time to go home. It was getting late. "Hi Mom!" said Jo as June opened the gate.

8

Next Jo and June went to visit Miss Annie. "Have some peaches," she said. "You both look quite hungry."

9

© Harcourt

One bright sunny day, Jo and June hurried out. "Let's go play by the pond!" Jo said with a shout.

"It's too cold to wade now," June said with a sigh. "Let's take a stroll and find something new to try."

"Thanks so much!" said the girls. "Thanks for the food." Jo and June were polite and never, ever rude.

Jo sat on the ground and cried, "Look what I've found!" June waved to a train that made a loud sound.

Cut-Out, Fold-Up Book 6 • Review

Directions: Help your child cut out and fold the book.